I hope
inspiration
these quotes

Rich

◆ FriesenPress

Suite 300 - 990 Fort St
Victoria, BC, V8V 3K2
Canada

www.friesenpress.com

Copyright © 2021 by Richard Cook
First Edition — 2021

All rights reserved.

No part of this publication may be reproduced in any form, or by any means, electronic or mechanical, including photocopying, recording, or any information browsing, storage, or retrieval system, without permission in writing from FriesenPress.

ISBN
978-1-5255-8454-1 (Hardcover)
978-1-5255-8455-8 (Paperback)
978-1-5255-8456-5 (eBook)

1. REFERENCE, QUOTATIONS

Distributed to the trade by The Ingram Book Company

DON'T QUOTE ME BUT...

RICHARD COOK

DEDICATION

What you hold in your hands now is years of hard work and countless hours finding, filing and sorting hundreds of quotes, sayings and blurbs. It has been a long road, at times a tedious journey that I have enjoyed every step of the way. This book is dedicated to three very special men.

My Dad, Walter Cook, always liked a wee smile and he could often be seen in the background with a wry grin on his face as the rest of us argued, discussed or diagnosed a subject. His German background was filled with witty sayings (some of which I can't repeat) and comical comments. He was my mentor, co-worker for many years, business partner and sounding post on many issues. He farmed all his life and had many opinions and sayings on many subjects. Dad instilled three things on us; faith, family and friends and as such that's where the funny, spiritual and philosophical quotes come from. Dad loved Christmas, as do I, and for this reason it's part of the book. I miss you everyday Pops. Have a Crown and Pepsi and enjoy it.

The other two men are fathers that I have never met but their hard work and dedication to raising a family is part of my life everyday. Lloyd May and Peter Robertson, you are missed.

All the quotes uncited in this book are anonymous, as most have been attributed to many different authors. All profits from this publication will go to three charities; The Princess Margaret Foundation, ALS Canada and the Canadian Cancer Association. I hope you enjoy looking through it as much as I have compiling it. Tell your friends about it because it is important to smile. So here we go, I'll start you with one of Dad's favorites;

Laugh and the world laughs with you, cry and you cry alone but walk around with a smirk on your face and you will confuse everyone.
Enjoy, Rich

FUNNY I

Whatever you do in life, always give 100%. Unless you are giving blood.
—MARTY ALLEN

Nothing is really lost until Mom can't find it.
—EVERYBODIES MOM

If you haven't grown up by age 50 you don't have too.
—DR. WHO

If people were meant to hop out of bed wide awake, they would sleep in a toaster.
—UNKNOWN

Women now have GPS and PMS. This means they will be grumpy when they find you.
—UNKNOWN

I don't have an attitude. I have a personality that you can't handle.
—TIMOTHY BENTKEY

I enjoy sarcasm because beating the crap out of people is illegal.
—R. STEVENS

To succeed in life you need three things; a wishbone, a backbone and a funnybone.
—ELAINE AGATHER

Some people need a sympathetic pat on the head… with a hammer…a big hammer.
—UNKNOWN

If I offended you with the opinions I voiced, you should be very concerned about the ones I kept to myself.
—GEORGE BUSH SR.

Sometimes I lay in bed at night and wonder, "where did I go wrong" and the little voice in my head says, "this will take more than one night".
—UNKNOWN

A good Mom lets you lick the beaters. A great Mom shuts the mixer off first.
—UNKNOWN

I'm not a complete idiot. Parts of me are missing.
—UNKNOWN

If you think you are too small to make a difference, try sleeping in the same room as a mosquito.
—MICHELLE WALKER

You can tell a lot about a woman by her hands. If she has them placed tightly around your neck she is probably upset.
—UNKNOWN

The fastest way to a man's heart is with a steak knife.
—ADRIENNE E. GUSOFF

Mankind has a perfect record while flying. We haven't left anyone up in the air yet.
—DOUGLAS ADAMS

The speed in which a woman says "nothing" is directly proportional to the incoming storm.
—SCOTTISH PROVERB

Speaking my mind is easy. Doing so tactfully, not so much.
—S. I. HAYAKAWA

I am responsible for what I say, not what you understand.
—PIERRE DE BEAUMARCHAIS

In Hollywood a marriage is a success if it outlasts milk.
—RITA RUDNER

Alcohol, because no good story ever started by the star eating salad.
—UNKNOWN

Some people think that tactics are a new kind of mint.
—UNKNOWN

Never tell a woman her diet isn't working.
—LYNN JOHNSON

I love my 6 pack abs so much that I protect them with a layer of fat.
—UNKNOWN

I don't suffer from insanity, I enjoy it.
—EDGAR ALLAN POE

Never argue with an idiot. They drag you down to their level and beat you with experience.
—JOHN GUERRERO

I started my life with nothing and still have most of it.
—LESLIE NIELSON

Don't kick me when I'm down because I will get up and then you are in trouble.
—VINCE LOMBARDI

Eagles may soar in the clouds but mice never get sucked into jet engines.
—JOHN BENFIELD

This could be a best selling country song. "If I'd have shot you sooner I'd be out by now".
—UNKNOWN

Some people say inappropriate things. I choose to call it vocal profiling.
—UNKNOWN

I had a wonderful evening. It wasn't tonight but I had one once.
—GROUCHO MARX

May those that love us, love us and those who don't love us let God turn their hearts. And if he can't turn their hearts may he turn their ankles so that we can tell who they are because of their limp.
—UNKNOWN

I never give the public hell. I tell them the truth and they think it is hell.
—HARRY S. TRUMAN

Do you know the reason people don't mind their own business. No mind, no business.
—WILLIAM S. BURROUGHS

Don't play stupid with me. I'm better at it than you are.
—UNKNOWN

Having one child makes you a parent. Having two or more makes you a referee.
—UNKNOWN

It's not a hangover. It's wine flu.
—HARVEY ALLEN

I don't have a problem with caffeine. I have a problem without it.
—UNKNOWN

Marriage is a relationship where one is always right and the other is a husband.
—TERRY PRATCHETT

When you really feel like slapping someone, do it and then yell "mosquito".
—UNKNOWN

I didn't lose my mind. It got scared and ran away.
—S. I. HAYAKAWA

You might say I'm insane but I prefer to call it mentally hilarious.
—JIMMY BUFFETT

Never trust a man who says he is the boss at home.
He probably lies about other stuff too.
—UNKNOWN

Time flies like an arrow. Fruit flies like a banana.
—GROUCHO MARX

A real man wants danger and play. That's why he
wants a woman.
—NORTHROP FRYE

To a pessimist a cup is half empty. To an optimist
it's half full. I like to think of it as room for
more rum.
—GEORGE CARLIN

You couldn't handle me even if I came
with instructions.
—HENRY FORD

I think my GPS broke. I was looking for Easy
Street and it sent me on the highway through Hell.
—OPRAH WINFREY

Gardening is cheaper than therapy and you get potatoes.
—ALFRED AUSTIN

Golf is a game where you yell fore, write down five and shoot six.
—WILL ROGERS

Needed immediately, a hammock and a winning lottery ticket.
—UNKNOWN

Handle stress like a dog. If you can't eat it or play with it, pee on it and walk away.
—HANS SELYE

Are humans the only mammals who are not afraid of vacuum cleaners.
—GARRISONKEILLOR

Contrary to popular belief, "Dammit" is not God's last name.
—UNKNOWN

Boobs are proof that men can concentrate on two things at once.
—UNKNOWN

One way to stop a fast horse from running is to bet on it.
—W. C. FIELDS

It doesn't matter if the glass is half full or half empty. There's room for more wine.
—GEORGE CARLIN

If I go and stand outside will you tell people I'm outstanding.
—MEREDITH WEST

I always mean what I say. Sometimes I don't mean to say it out loud.
—KATHERINE HEIGL

Whenever I get a headache, I take two aspirins and stay away from small children, just like it says on the bottle.
—ERMA BOMBECK

A backward poet writes inverse.
—FREDRICK

A river valley is absolutely gorges.
—UNKNOWN

The problem with the gene pool is that there is no lifeguard.
—STEVEN WRIGHT

Some drink from the fountain of youth while others only gargle.
—GRANT M. BRIGHT

Be careful when reading health books. You could die of a misprint.
—MARK TWAIN

I don't drink alcohol, I drink spirits. Therefore I am not an alcoholic, I'm a spiritualist.
—UNKNOWN

I'm sleepy. Is there an app for that.
—FRAN LEBOWICH

The older you get, the less important it becomes to act your age.
—NORMAN VINCENT PEALE

A positive attitude will not solve all your problems but it will annoy enough people to make it worth the effort.
—HERM ALBRIGHT

I ask God for a bike but I know he doesn't work like that so I stole a bike and ask for forgiveness.
—EMO PHILLIPS

The last thing I want to do is hurt you but, remember it still is on the list.
—UNKNOWN

I didn't fight my way to the top of the food chain to become a vegetarian.
—UNKNOWN

Why do people believe you when you say there are 4 billion stars in the sky but, when you say "wet paint" they still have to touch it.
—UNKNOWN

Some people make happiness wherever they go, others whenever they go.
—OSCAR WILDE

Never hit a man with glasses. Use a chair instead.
—ROSEANNE BARR

Money talks but all mine says is goodbye.
—RICHARD ARMOUR

When you choke a smurf, what color does it turn.
—UNKNOWN

It's called Tourist Season so do you need a special hunting license.
—UNKNOWN

Alcohol doesn't solve everything but neither does milk.
—UNKNOWN

If corn oil comes from corn, where does baby oil come from.
—UNKNOWN

Think how stupid the average person is and then realize that 50% of the population is stupider than that.
—HOMER SIMPSON

Beer doesn't have many vitamins in it, that's why you have to drink alot of it.
—UNKNOWN

Grammar is the difference between feeling you're nuts and feeling your nuts.
—E. B. WHITE

If money doesn't grow on trees, why do banks have branches.
—AMERICAN PROVERB

A woman without curves is like a road without bends. You get there faster but the ride is boring.
—CHARLES KURALT

Change is inevitable, except from a vending machine.
—ROBERT C. GALLAGHER

Middle age is when your age starts to show around the middle.
—BOB HOPE

A word to the wise isn't necessary. It's the dumb ones that need advice.
—BILL COSBY

Before marriage a man yearns for the woman he loves. After marriage the "y" is silent.
—W. A. CLARKE

Is popcorn a vegetable.
—UNKNOWN

It has been said that people cause accidents. The reverse is true also.
—ELIE WIESEL

Don't marry for money. It's cheaper to borrow from the bank.
—SCOTTISH PROVERB

I wish I was a glow worm, as a glow worm is never glum, cause how can you be grumpy when the sun shines out your bum.
—UNKNOWN

We are born wet, naked and hungry, and then things get worse.
—LILY TOMLIN

I didn't lose my mind. I sold it on Ebay.
—P. J. ROURKE

Does fuzzy logic tickle.
—UNKNOWN

Is the ethernet something you use to catch the ether bunny.
—UNKNOWN

She had a face like a Saint…Bernard.
—GROUCHO MARX

Politics is the second oldest profession on earth and it's eerily similar to the oldest profession.
—RONALD REAGAN

You only need a parachute if you want to skydive twice.
—SCOTT ADAMS

If winning isn't everything, why do we keep score.
—VINCE LOMBARDI

When chemists die, do they barium.
—UNKNOWN

I stayed up all night to see where the sun went and then it dawned on me.
—UNKNOWN

I tried to catch some fog and mist.
—UNKNOWN

I once dated an Irish woman. I think she was after my lucky charms.
—UNKNOWN

Even duct tape can't fix stupid.
—JEFFERY VEEN

I was out drinking on St. Patrick's Day and took the bus home. That might not seem like a big deal to you but I had never driven a bus before.
—UNKNOWN

SPIRITUAL QUOTES

The happiest people don't have the best of everything....they make the best of everything.
—WILLIAM LYON PHELPS

THE GIFT OF LIFE IS YOURS TO BORROW.
—JOHNATHON LARSON

If you want something you have never had you must do something you've never done.
—JANE GOODALL

Your beliefs don't make you a better person. Your behavior does.
—MAHATMA GANDHI

When you feel like you are drowning in life's problems, don't worry, your lifeguard can walk on water.
—UNKNOWN

THOSE WE LOVE DON'T GO AWAY, THEY WALK BESIDE US EVERYDAY. UNSEEN, UNHEARD BUT ALWAYS NEAR. SO LOVED, SO MISSED, SO EVER DEAR.
—MAURICE MAETERLINCK

Wherever you go and whatever you do, do it with all your heart.
—THOMAS KEMPIS

What if today we were just grateful for everything.
—J. C. PENNEY

Your time is precious. Don't waste it on someone who doesn't realize that you are too.
—BENJAMIN DISRAELIAE

There is always something to be thankful for.
—IZAAC WALTON

One day you will just be a memory. Make it a good one.
—EDWARD DE BONO

To love someone deeply gives you strength, to be loved deeply gives you courage.
—ELIZABETH BOWEN

You can't shake hands with a clenched fist.
—INDIRA GANDHI

Let us live so that when we die even the undertaker is sad.
—MARK TWAIN

Love the random memories that make you smile no matter what is going on in your life right now.
—OLIVER WENDALL HOLMES

When life puts you in difficult situations, instead of saying "Why me" say "Try me".
—ARTHUR ASHE

Dear God; Why do you allow such violence in our schools. Concerned Parent. Dear Concerned Parent; Don't blame me I'm not allowed in schools. God
—UNKNOWN

Mankind judges you by your belief in God. God judges you by your belief in mankind.
—CHAPMAN COHEN

A teardrop landing on your cheek is a kiss from someone who lives in heaven and is watching over you.
—UNKNOWN

Tomorrow is never promised, so be nice, kind and thankful today.
—BIBLE

Sometimes it's not the song that makes you emotional, it's the people and memories that come to mind when you hear the song.
—PHILIP ROTH

Worry will not empty tomorrow of its troubles, it will only empty today of its strength.
—BO BENNETT

One small positive thought first thing in the morning, can change your whole day.
—ROBERT H. SCHULLER

Everything will be alright in the end, so, if everything is not alright it isn't the end yet.
—MITCH ALBOM

You are given three gifts; life, love and understanding. Use them.
—FRENCH LAW

When life is sweet say thank you and celebrate. When life is bitter say thank you and grow.
—RALPH WALDO EMERSON

Grief is the price we pay for love.
—PROVERB

Don't strive to make your presence noticed, strive to make your absence felt.
—MICHAEL HAINEY

When the power of love overtakes the love of power we will know peace.
—WILLIAM EWART GLADSTONE

Never worry about the numbers. Help one person at a time and always start with those nearest to you.
—MOTHER TERESA

When you put faith, hope and love together, you can raise positive kids in a negative world.
—ZIG ZIGLAR

Love all, trust few and do wrong to no one.
—WILLIAM SHAKESPEARE

The first wealth is health.
—GEORGE HERBERT

The one that follows the crowd will find himself no further than the crowd. The one who walks alone will find himself where no one has ever been.
—UNKNOWN

I'm not saying life is going to be easy. I'm saying it's going to be worth it.
—HENRY FORD

People don't find willpower and strength. They create it.
—MARCIA WIEDER

Never let success go to your head or failure go to your heart.
—DAVID FEHERTY

We do not need an intelligent mind that speaks, we need a patient heart that listens.
—BASIL S. WALSH

Five simple rules for life; free your heart from hatred, free your mind from worries, live simply, give more and expect less.
—GEORGE BERNARD SHAW

Going to church doesn't anymore make you a Christian than standing in a garage makes you a car.
—UNKNOWN

Don't worry who your kids grow up to be. Worry about who they grow up to be like.
—UNKNOWN

Forgiveness does not change the past but it enlarges the future.
—PAUL BOESE

No matter how far wrong you've gone in life, you can always turn around.
—MARTIN LUTHER KING JR.

I WISH THERE WERE VISITING HOURS
IN HEAVEN.
—UNKNOWN

When you are always ahead of the others you always walk alone.
—PROVERB

Never drive faster than your Guardian Angel can fly.
—UNKNOWN

When you kill time, you injure eternity.
—HENRY DAVID THOREAU

Be less interested in "why you are here" and more interested in "While you are here".
—UNKNOWN

A good life is when you assume nothing, do more, need less, smile often, dream big, laugh lots and realize how blessed you are.
—BERTRAND RUSSELL

Courage is fear that has said its prayers.
—DOROTHY BERNARD

Live in such a way that, if someone speaks badly of you no one will believe them.
—BERTRAND RUSSELL

The trouble is you think you have time.
—ANTHONY D'ANGELO

Sometimes I open my mouth and my father comes out.
—UNKNOWN

I want to be your favorite hello and your hardest goodbye.
—UNKNOWN

Do not regret growing old. It is a privilege denied to many.
—ANDRE MAUROIS

The most precious jewellery you can have around your neck is the arms of a child.
—MARK TWAIN

We must be our own before we can be someone else's.
—SALLY FIELD

You have two hands. One to help yourself and one to help others.
—BILLY GRAHAM

It might not be today, tomorrow or the next day but everything will be alright.
—BILLY GRAHAM

If life gets too hard to stand…kneel.
—UNKNOWN

If you die in an elevator, make sure you push the "Up" button.
—UNKNOWN

As long as you remember that God is there for you it doesn't matter who is against you.
—JOHN HAGGAI

Sometimes rock bottom is the perfect spot to start and rebuild.
—ARTHUR MILLER

Pray the hardest when it is the hardest to pray.
—MARTIN LUTHER

Even the darkest hour only has 60 minutes.
—PROVERB

Nothing matters very much and few things matter at all.
—ARTHUR BALFOUR

Every saint has a past and every sinner has a future.
—OSCAR WILDE

Sometimes memories sneak out my eyes and down my cheeks.
—HEINRICH HEINE

Respect and trust are free gifts within you to give.
—REN

If you are going through hell, keep going.
—SIR WINSTON CHURCHILL

Precious moments are the molecules that make up eternity.
—WIEDER MARCIA

Talent is a gift but character is a choice.
—MARY LOU RETTON

Always give the ones you love wings to fly, roots to come back to and reasons to stay.
—WILLIAM HOLDING CARTER JR.

Never give up on dreams because of the time they will take. That time will pass anyway.
—TOM BRADLEY

Dear God, sometimes I don't have words for my prayers. Please listen to my heart.
—DANIEL WEBSTER

When you can't find the sunshine, be the sunshine.
—JANIS BARRIE

Think in years, work in days and live in the moment.
—UNKNOWN

There are lots of people that would love to have your bad days.
—WOODROW WILSON

DON'T QUOTE ME BUT...

I opened two gifts this morning. My eyes.
—SYLVIA PLATH

Just love everyone, God will sort it out later.
—WAYNE DYER

PHILOSOPHICAL QUOTES

Don't do something permanently stupid because you are temporarily upset.
—MARCUS AURELIUS

Sometimes I expect more of you because I am willing to do that much more for you.
—PHIL NEVILLE

Common sense is a flower that doesn't grow in everyone's garden.
—VOLTAIRE

If you want to go fast, go alone. If you want to go far, go with others.
—UNKNOWN

Hugs were invented to let special people know you love them without saying a word.
—RALPH WALDO EMERSON

Believe that you can and you are halfway there.
—DAVID ZUCKER

When I am happy and cheerful my friends know who I am. When I am sad and depressed I know who my friends are.
—LALAINE

The greatest challenge in life is finding out who you are. The second greatest challenge is being happy with what you find.
—ZIG ZIGLAR

Don't fear change, change fear.
—ANTHONY J. D'ANGELO

Holding a grudge is letting someone live rent free inside your head.
—BUDDY HACKETT

Every accomplishment comes with a decision to try.
—JOHANN VON GOETHE

If you want your place in the sun, you have to put up with a few blisters.
—LORETTA YOUNG

To succeed you have to believe in something with such passion that it becomes reality.
—DAVID VISCOTT

Never put your key to happiness in someone else's pocket.
—W. R. INGE

Sarcasm is the brains defense against the less intelligent.
—FYODOR DOSTOYEVSKY

The trouble with trouble is that it starts out being so much fun.
—QUINCY JONES

You cannot live a positive life with a negative mind.
—MATTHIEU RICARD

If you have enemies, that is good. It means you stood up for something important at some point in your life.
—WINSTON CHURCHILL

Don't look back, you are not going that way.
—HUGH WHITE

A new year is a clean slate to write your 365 day story on.
—OPRAH WINFREY

A bend in the road is not the end of the road unless you fail to make the turn.
—ROBERT H. SCHULLER

Always go the extra mile. The road is never crowded.
—WAYNE DYER

Whether you think you can or you can't, you are right.
—MARY KAY ASH

Don't dwell on who let you down, dwell on who helped you back up.
—TECH N9NE

Never let your schooling interfere with your education.
—LEE IACOCCA

Being defeated is temporary, giving up is permanent.
—THOMAS EDISON

Sometimes you have to forget what you feel and remember what you deserve.
—DALE MURPHY

As we grow older we realize it is less important to have more friends and more important to have real ones.
—YOLANDA HADID

It is never too late to be what you might have been.
—GEORGE ELIOT

If you choose the lesser of two evils, remember you are still choosing evil.
—MAX LERNER

You cannot build a reputation on what you are going to do.
—LIZ SMITH

When in doubt, tell the truth.
—DAVID MAMET

It's not what you look at, it's what you see.
—HENRY DAVID THOREAU

Mother's are like buttons. They hold everything together.
—JULIETTE BINOCHE

If you aim for nothing in life, you will have amazing accuracy.
—FLORENCE SCOVEL SCHINN

Success is something you attract by the person you become.
—GEORGE S. PATTON

Some people enter your life as a blessing, others as a life lesson.
—JOHN W. GARDINER

If we did all the things we are capable of, we would astound ourselves.
—FLORENCE SCOVEL SCHINN

Today's mighty oak is yesterday's acorn that held its ground.
—UNKNOWN

Live like somebody left the gate open.
—SUHASINI MANIRATNAM

Success is not the key to happiness, happiness is the key to success.
—ALBERT SCHWEITZER

I might not be there yet but I'm closer than I was yesterday.
—ROBERT ORBEN

Last words are for fools that haven't said enough.
—LES DAWSON

Success is a matter of hanging on after everyone else has let go.
—WILLIAM FEATHER

Do what you can, with what you have, where you are.
—THEODORE ROOSEVELT

When you stop chasing the wrong things, you give the right things a chance to catch you.
—WILLIAM MOULTON MARSTON

You miss 100% of the shots you do not take.
—MICHAEL JORDAN

The real measure of your worth would be how much you are worth if you lost all your money.
—UNKNOWN

Life is short, smile while you still have teeth.
—JEFF ROSS

Don't fear your abilities, fear your mind. That's what gets in the way of success.
—ANTHONY D'ANGELO

Some people find fault like there was a reward for it.
—HENRY FORD

The great thing about rumors are that you get to learn alot about yourself that you didn't already know.
—UNKNOWN

Every accomplishment starts with the decision to try.
—UNKNOWN

Love is a trick played on mankind to ensure the continuation of our species.
—UNKNOWN

The greatest things in life are done little by little.
—IDRIES SHAH

I would rather live a life of "Oh wells" than "What ifs".
—ROBBY GORDON

My daily routine is; get up, be amazing, go back to bed.
—MIKE MURDOCK

Life doesn't happen to you, it responds to you.
—LOU HOLTZ

Tough times don't last, tough people do.
—ROBERT H. SCHULER

Character is how you treat someone who can do nothing for you.
—ARISTOTLE

If your dog doesn't like someone, you probably shouldn't either.
—KRISTIN DAVIS

Spend time with the ones that you love or else you will end up saying "I wish I had" instead of "I'm glad I did".
—JOHN LONGDEN

Be like a lit candle, it can light thousands of other candles without shortening its own life.
—BUDDHA

Happiness does not decrease by being shared.
—RALPH WALDO EMERSON

Sometimes I feel like throwing in the towel but that would only make more work.
—GEORGE BERNARD SHAW

You are not defeated when you lose, you are defeated when you quit.
—RICHARD M. NIXON

Be careful who you share your secrets with, there are only a few who care and the rest are only curious.
—CHANAKYA

If you don't have time to do it right, when will you have time to do it again.
—RAVYN LENAE

Live your life and forget your age.
—NORMAN VINCENT PEALE

Marriage is the opportunity to inherit an additional dysfunctional family just in case the one you have is not enough.
—UNKNOWN

Somewhere something incredible is going to happen. Do it.
—CARL SAGAN

There is no such thing as a small act of kindness.
—SCOTT ADAMS

Any fool can paint a picture but it takes a wise man to be able to sell it.
—THOMAS FULLER

Life is like a combination lock, your job is to find the right numbers, in the right order and then you can have anything you want.
—LUDWIG WITTGENSTEIN

It is not a sin to pay yourself a compliment.
—MARK TWAIN

You can because you think you can.
—HENRY FORD

A professional is someone who does his best at a time that he doesn't want to.
—ALLISTAIR COOKE

It is better to fail in honor than to thrive among cheats.
—HERMAN MEVILLE

When your work speaks for itself, don't interrupt.
—HENRY J. KAISER

Flowers say what the heart is too full to express.
—HENRY DAVID THOREAU

You can't depend on your eyes if your imagination is out of focus.
—MARK TWAIN

If there are no ups and downs in your life, you are dead.
—JAMI GERTZ

One of the hardest decisions in life is whether to walk away or try harder.
—MICHAEL JORDAN

You have not lived until you do something for someone who cannot repay you.
—JOHN WOODEN

It is difficult to see the whole picture when you always want to be inside the frame.
—HELEN HAYES

Put your hand on a hot stove and it will feel like an hour. Sit beside a pretty woman for an hour and it will feel like a second. That's reality.
—ALBERT EINSTEIN

Advice from a tree; stand tall and proud, go out on a limb, remember your roots, drink plenty of water, be content with your natural beauty and enjoy the view.
—PROVERB

We make a living by what we get. We make a life by what we give.
—ARTHUR ASHE

Work for the cause not the applause.
—DESIDERIUS ERASMUS

Live life to express not impress.
—WILLIAM AMES

Be the change you want to see in the world.
—VICTORIA OSTEEN

Motivation doesn't last but neither does bathing. That's why we need both daily.
—ZIG ZIGLAR

Mothers of little boys live from son up to son down.
—UNKNOWN

Judging a person does not define who they are, it defines who you are.
—CAL LE MON

On the other hand you have different fingers.
—STEVEN WRIGHT

Yesterday is a cancelled cheque, tomorrow is a promissory note, today is cash so spend it wisely.
—HANK STRAM

A halo only has to drop a few inches to become
a noose.
—PROVERB

The difference between genius and stupidity is that
genius has its limits.
—UNKNOWN

Always drink upstream from the herd.
—W. C. FIELDS

Life is an echo, what you send out comes
right back.
—ADAGE

He who hesitates is probably right.
—BOGOVICH

An intellectual is someone who has found
something more interesting than sex.
—ALDOUS HUXELY

A real man treats his woman the same way he
wants a young man to treat his daughter.
—ROBERT JOHNSON

Trying to be happy by accumulating possessions is like trying to satisfy your hunger by taping food to your body.
—UNKNOWN

Don't find fault. Find a remedy.
—HENRY FORD

Be yourself, the original is always worth more than a copy.
—FRANK J. GIBLIN

The harder you work, the luckier you are.
—SAMUEL GOLDWYN

Gravity cannot be held responsible for people falling in love.
—ALBERT EINSTEIN

A man who does not read books has no advantage over a man who cannot read.
—MARK TWAIN

Everyone is gifted but only a few unwrap the whole gift.
—ANDRE GIDE

You can't cross the ocean by staring at the water.
—RABINDRANATH TAGORE

Time is a great healer but a lousy beautician.
—LUCILLE S. HARPER

Children need to be taught how to think, not what to think.
—JOHN DEWEY

You don't need someone to complete you. you need someone to accept you completely.
—KEN KEYES JR.

When you reach the top, keep climbing.
—J. PAUL GETTY

Don't expect everyone to understand your journey, especially if they have never walked on your path.
—GITA BELLIN

The past is where you learn the lesson. The future is where you apply it.
—DONALD TRUMP

It is much easier to be critical then to be correct.
—BENJAMIN DISRAELI

Your beliefs don't make you a better person, your behavior does.
—SHARON ANTHONY BOWER

I have an interest in the future because I'm going to spend the rest of my life there.
—CHARLES FRANKLIN KETTERING

Don't educate your children to be rich, educate them to be happy. So that when they grow up they know the value of things and not the price.
—ANDREW SOLOMON

Being happy does not mean everything is perfect, it means that I have decided to look past the imperfections.
—JENNIE JEROME CHURCHILL

There are seven days in a week and someday is not one of them.
—UNKNOWN

One of the happiest moments in life is when you find the courage to let go of the things you cannot change.
—ERICH FROMM

Everyday cannot be good but there can be good in every day.
—HORACE

Being happy does not mean everything is good. It means you have found the right medication.
—CARRIE WILSON

Music washes away the dust of everyday life from your soul.
—BERTHOLD AUERBACH

You can do anything but not everything.
—JOHN W. GARDNER

It only takes one person to change your life...you.
—PAUL ARDEN

Enjoy life, it's not a dress rehearsal.
—ROSE TREMAIN

Sometimes it's better to be kind than right.
—ENGLISH PROVERB

One of the greatest feelings in life is when you hug someone you love and they hug you back even harder.
—UNKNOWN

The past cannot be changed but the future is within your power.
—MARY PICKFORD

Courage does not always roar. Sometimes it's a quiet voice at the end of the day that says, "Let's try again tomorrow".
—JOSE CAULDERON

Light travels faster than sound. That's why some people seem to be intelligent until they speak.
—UNKNOWN

We never grow up, we just learn how to act in public.
—BRYAN WHITE

Knowledge is knowing a tomato is a fruit. Wisdom is not putting it in fruit salad.
—BRIAN O'DRISCOLL

The early bird might get the worm but the second mouse gets the cheese.
—JEREMY PAXMAN

When in doubt…mumble.
—JAMES H. BOREN

Worrying works because 90% of the things I worry about never happen.
—BILL PARCELLS

Nostalgia isn't what it used to be.
—PETER DE VRIES

Some mistakes are too much fun to only make once.
—UNKNOWN

You know your chiildren are growing up when they quit asking where they came from and won't tell you where they are going.
—JOHN PLOMP

If you can't convince them, confuse them.
—HARRY S. TRUMAN

Progress is made by lazy people trying to find an easier way to do things.
—ROBERT A HEINLEIN

We are all time travellers travelling at the speed of 60 seconds per minute.
—CHRISTINE WARREN

The difference between fiction and reality is that fiction has to make sense.
—TOM CLANCY

Not everything that can be counted counts and not everything that counts can be counted.
—ALBERT EINSTEIN

Life is better when you are laughing.
—AUDREY HEPBURN

In youth we learn and in age we understand.
—MARIE E. ESCHENBACH

Success is the sum of small efforts, repeated day in and day out.
—ROBERT COLLIER

When nothing goes right, go left.
—UNKNOWN

Don't kiss at the garden gate, love is blind but the neighbors ain't.
—D. H. LAWRENCE

Flying is just learning how to fall without hitting the ground.
—DOUGLAS ADAMS

Teachers call it cheating. Students call it teamwork.
—TERRY PRATCHETT

If swimming is so good for you, explain the size of whales.
—IRISH MUSING

When you speak with your eyes you tell more than one story.
—YIDDISH PROVERB

All reports are in. Life is not always fair.
—JOEL OSTEEN

No snowflake in an avalanche ever feels responsible.
—STANISLAW LEC

Education is what you get from reading the fine print. Experience is what you get when you don't read it.
—UNKNOWN

For every mile of road you drive there are two miles of ditch.
—HENRY FORD

When you talk to your kids remember, it's rain that grows flowers, not thunder.
—MARK TWAIN

Don't jus teach your kids how to count but what counts as well.
—ARISTOTLE ONASSIS

We can't choose the music that life deals us but we can choose how we dance to that music.
—GARY CHAPMAN

Don't judge the day by the crop that you reap but instead by the seeds that you sow.
—INDIAN PROVERB

Never confuse education with intelligence.
—BENJAMIN FRANKLIN

Philosophy is a route of many roads that leads from nowhere to nothing.
—AMBROSE BIERCE

Be better than you were yesterday.
—WILLIAM FAULKNER

Minds are like parachutes, they only work when they are open.
—LORD THOMAS DEWAR

A goal without a plan is just a wish.
—BO BENNETT

Failure is success if we learn from it.
—MALCOLM STEVENSON FORBES

The best way to cheer yourself up is to cheer up those around you.
—MARK TWAIN

Success comes from cans. Failure comes from can'ts.
—JOHN WOODEN

Half the people in the world are below average.
—STUART BOARD

Love is grand, divorce is 200 grand.
—JOAN RIVERS

Life is tough, wear a helmet.
—BOBBY SHORT

Everyone has a photographic memory. Some just don't have any film.
—DAVE BARRY

Just because no one complains doesn't mean everything is okay. Think about a broken parachute.
—BENNY HILL

If you stumble, make it part of the dance.
—DENNIS WAITLEY

There is no elevator to success, you must take the stairs.
—JOE GIRARD

Be the kind of person you want to meet.
—RENEE RUSSO

The only person you need to be better than is the person you were yesterday.
—WILLIAM FAULKNER

Life doesn't always introduce you to the people you want to meet.
—HORACE

Everyone has a purpose in life even if it is to be a bad example.
—WAYNE DYER

Life is like a roll of toilet paper, long and useful.
—ALICIA SILVERSTONE

Strive for progress, not perfection.
—ROBERT F. KENNEDY

A good deed brightens a dark world.
—VINCENT VAN GOGH

To be in your children's memories tomorrow, you have to be in their lives today.
—DEBRA STEPHENSON

Be so happy that when others look at you, they become happy too.
—ANNE FRANK

You were born to make an impact.
—JOHN H. HOLCOMB

Childhood is a wonderful time when all you need to do to lose weight is to take a bath.
—UNKNOWN

The sooner you fall behind, the more time you have to catch up.
—UNKNOWN

Experience is something you don't get until right after you need it.
—STEVEN WRIGHT

You can't be late until you show up.
—UNKNOWN

Why fit in when you were born to stand out.
—MEREDITH WEST

Flattery is like cologne water, smelled but not swallowed.
—JOSH BILLINGS

Tact is the art of making a point without making an enemy.
—HOWARD W. NEWTON

Broken pencils are pointless.
—MIKE CERNOVICH

Sometimes you win, sometimes you learn.
—LOU HOLTZ

A bad attitude is like a flat tire, you can't go anywhere until you change it.
—ADAGE

To be old and wise you must first be young and stupid.
—BILLY OCEAN

Some days you are the pain and other days you are the a@#.
—LIFE LESSON

Our age is simply the number of years others have been enjoying us.
—INDIAN PROVERB

Happiness is not a destination, it's a way of life.
—HAIM GINOTT

I don't want a happy ending. I want a never ending.
—HERBERT SPENSER

Memories take us back and dreams take us forward.
—JEREMY IRONS

When was the last time you did something for the first time.
—LYNWOOD L. GIACOMINI

Intelligence without ambition is like a bird without wings.
—C. ARCHIE DANIELSON

Love is acting stupid together.
—E. JOSEPH COSSMAN

A smile is the most beautiful curve on a woman's body.
—PHYLLIS DILLER

I'm not weird, I'm limited edition.
—TIMBALAND

Write your troubles in sand and your blessings in stone.
—ARABIC PROVERB

A home becomes a castle when the king and queen are in love.
—BLAISE PASCAL

If not now...when.
—MARTIN LUTHER

Love is a friendship set on fire.
—LORD BYRON

If you don't want anybody else to find out about it, don't do it.
—JOE DI MAGGIO

No one looks back on their life and remembers the nights they had plenty of sleep.
—W. C. FIELDS

If the music in your head is good...dance.
—ALAN WATTS

The word "listen" contains the same letters as "silent".
—UNKNOWN

Some people feel the rain while others just get wet.
—INDIAN PROVERB

Follow your heart but take your brains along.
—J. COLE

The bad news is that time flies. The good news is that you are the pilot.
—ROBERT ORBEN

Don't raise your voice, improve your argument.
—ZENDAYA

Love what you have and remember what you have had.
—HOWARD COSELL

Be kind whenever possible and it is always possible.
—BIBLE

You only live once but if you do it right, once is enough.
—JOE E. LEWIS

Mistakes are part of the dues we pay for a full life.
—ROBERT GALVIN

It is better to have one friend of great value than many friends of little value.
—ESTER M. CLARK

The purpose of life is life with a purpose.
—ROBERT BYRNE

You cannot solve your problems with the same thinking that you used to create them.
—BETTY DE VOS

If you cut too many corners, you will end up going in circles.
—FRANK DANE

A drunk mans words are a sober mans thoughts.
—ERNEST HEMINGWAY

Luck is what is left when you give 100%.
—ELMER G. LETTERMAN

If you think education is difficult, try being stupid.
—UNKNOWN

Age is the price we pay for maturity.
—TOM STOPPARD

If you can't see the bright side of life, polish the dull side.
—RUMI

Always remember you are unique, just like everybody else.
—T. S. ELIOT

"How are you" is a greeting, not a question.
—UNKNOWN

Women who want to be equal to men lack ambition.
—TIMOTHY LEARY

An expert in anything was once a beginner
—BARBARA SHER

Children will soon forget your presents and long remember your presence.
—WAYNE DYER

The only thing that matters is the effort.
—WILLIAM OLSER

There is a reason the rear view mirror is smaller than the windshield.
—JOSH BOWMAN

Of course exercise burns, but complaining won't make you look good naked.
—RICHARD SIMMONS

Make sure your own worst enemy is not living between your ears.
—LOUIS BINSTOCK

You can be the ripest, juiciest peach on the tree but there are still going to be people who don't like peaches.
—DENZEL WASHINGTON

Don't give up what you want most for what you want now.
—ELLA FITZGERALD

Some people are so poor, all they have is money.
—IMELDA MARCOS

If we don't feel grateful for what we have, what makes us think we would be grateful if we had more.
—BASIL S. WALSH

Bloom where you were planted.
—GEORGE SANTAYANA

Worrying is like a rocking chair, it gives you something to do but you don't get anywhere.
—GYPSY ROSE LEE

If you want to come into my life, the door is open. If you want out of my life, the door is open. Just one request, don't stand in the doorway and block traffic.
—UNKNOWN

Life is about using the whole box of crayons.
—BARBARA CORCORAN

What really matters in life is rarely on the "to do" list.
—SHIRLEY LORD

People are sent into our lives to make us learn about ourselves.
—TATIANA MASLANY

Some of the best days of your life haven't happened yet.
—W. SOMERSET MAUGHAM

Learn to love the skies you are under.
—SIR ARTHUR KENT

Promote what you love instead of bashing what you hate.
—ISRAEL SALANTER

Life has no remote. You have to change it yourself.
—JILLIAN MICHAELS

Your mood should not dictate your manners.
—RICHARD WHATLEY

Chocolate doesn't ask silly questions. Chocolate understands totally.
—ELAINE SHERMAN

Storms make trees take deeper roots.
—GEORGE HERBERT

There are good days and there are bad days. This is one of them. Your choice.
—BILLY JOEL

Life is like a game of poker, if you don't put anything in the pot you can't take anything out.
—WILLIAM CHRISTOPHER HANDY

Life is more like a cobweb than an organizational chart.
—ROSS PEROT

The day after tomorrow is the third day of the rest of your life.
—GEORGE BURNS

Never let yesterday use up too much of today.
—INDIAN PROVERB

Life is like ice cream, enjoy before it melts away.
—CHARLES M. SHULTZ

The best use of your life is to invest in something that will outlast your life.
—FRANK LLOYD WRIGHT

You can't have everything. Where would you put it.
—STEVEN WRIGHT

Integrity is doing the right thing even though no one is watching.
—VICTOR HUGO

Knowledge is power but enthusiasm works the switch.
—IVERN BALL

We are a perishable item. Live accordingly.
—OVID

Don't let what you cannot do interfere with what you can do.
—LUCILLE BALL

Lifes burdens are lighter when you can laugh at yourself.
—GILLIAN ANDERSON

Worrying will not stop the bad stuff from happening, it just stops you from enjoying the good stuff.
—MATT BONDI

Laugh when you can, apologize when you should and let go of what you cannot change.
—PEACE PILGRIM

Dogs laugh with their tails.
—MAX EASTMAN

Many pieces of music finish long after they end.
—IGOR STRAVINSKY

Life can only be understood backwards but must be lived forwards.
—SOREN KIERKEGAARD

It doesn't matter how often a married man changes jobs, he still has the same boss.
—DAVE BARRY

Facts do not cease just because they are ignored.
—ALDOUS HUXLEY

Doing more things faster is no substitute for doing them right.
—A. J. LIEBLING

If you don't know where you are going you might end up somewhere else.
—PETER LAWRENCE

I don't know the key to success but the key to failure is trying to please everybody.
—BILL COSBY

We can draw lessons from the past but we cannot live in it.
—RONALD REAGAN

Siblings are different flowers from the same garden.
—MARGHERITA MISSONI

Reading a good book won't solve all your problems but neither will housework.
—ERMA BOMBECK

Just because you can doesn't mean you should.
—PROVERB

Nothing is foolproof to a sufficiently talented fool.
—GENE BROWN

It's always a good day to have a good day.
—UNKNOWN

Don't think about the future, it will come soon enough.
—ALBERT EINSTEIN

A word to the wise isn't necessary, it's the stupid ones that need advice.
—BILL COSBY

Marriages are made in heaven but so is thunder and lightning.
—CLINT EASTWOOD

You don't have to worry about the whole staircase, just the next step.
—DAS HAMMARSKJOLD

Learning is a gift even if the teacher is a pain.
—ERIC ALLENBAUGH

If I am driving you crazy make sure to put on your seatbelt.
—DOUG HORTON

The squeaky wheel doesn't always get the grease. Sometimes it gets replaced.
—UNKNOWN

The voices in my head are arguing about who gets to be me today.
—UNKNOWN

Nothing but the future lies ahead.
—PAUL PAULSEN

It never rains on a dry day.
—UNKNOWN

When life hands you lemons don't be afraid to say "No thank you".
—HENRY ROLLINS

Optimism has no inhibitions based on past experiences.
—NORMAN COUSINS

Courage is what it takes to stand up and speak but courage is also what it takes to sit down and listen.
—AMBROSE REDMOON

Life was much simpler when "Apple" and "Blackberry" were fruits.
—STEVE JOBS

You are never too old to set a new goal or dream a new dream.
—CARL SANDBURG

You live longer once you realize that any time spent being unhappy is time wasted.
—DR. JAMES A. WALSH

If you can't be positive at least be quiet.
—MARIAN WRIGHT EDELMAN

They gave their tomorrow so we could have our today.
—A. P. J. ABDUL-KALAM

I'm not where I need to be but I'm not where I used to be.
—MAX DE PREE

Hard work beats talent when talent doesn't work hard.
—ROBERT HALF

There are no bad days when you come home to a dogs love.
—UNKNOWN

Life always offers you a second chance. It's called tomorrow.
—BRIGHAM YOUNG

Move different if you want different. Old keys can't open new doors.
—MAXWELL MALTZ

Home is not a place, it's a feeling.
—PLINY THE ELDER

Sometimes life feels like a test that I didn't study for.
—ERIC CANTONA

When life closes one door, open another one. That's how doors work.
—UNKNOWN

Blowing out somebody else's candle doesn't make yours shine any brighter.
—MIDRASH

Stay away from negative people, they have a problem for every solution.
—ROBERT ZEND

Be the person your dog thinks you are.
—WAYNE DYER

When life knocks you down, roll over and look at the stars.
—LES BROWN

My reality cheque bounced.
—ERMA BOMBECK

Why limit "happy" to just one hour.
—UNKNOWN

When life throws you a rainy day, play in the puddles.
—FRAN LEBOWITZ

Your speed doesn't matter. Forward is forward.
—TYGA

They told me I couldn't. That's why I did.
—JONATHAN WINTERS

CHRISTMAS QUOTES

Do you call people that are afraid of Christmas Claustrophobic.
—UNKNOWN

Maybe Christmas doesn't come from a store. Maybe its meaning is a little bit more.
—HOW THE GRINCH STOLE CHRISTMAS

It's not what's under the tree that matters. It's who is around it.
—JOSIE BISSETT

There are two things to give your kids each Christmas. One is roots and the other is wings.
—WILLIAM HOLDING CARTER JR.

Keep your Christmas heart open all year long.
—UNKNOWN

Which Christmas is the most vivid for me.
Next Christmas.
—UNKNOWN

At Christmastime all roads lead to home.
—AMBROSE BIERCE

Love is what is left under the tree when you are done opening and you listen.
—BRIAN SUTTON SMITH

Remember next December that love weighs more than gold.
—UNKNOWN

Christmas should be less about opening presents and more about opening hearts.
—JESSE JACKSON

The true meaning of Christmas is that we are never alone.
—RACHEL CARSON

As long as we know in our hearts what Christmas ought to be, Christmas is.
—UNKNOWN

There are no strangers on Christmas Eve.
—UNKNOWN

There is nothing sadder in this world than to wake up on Christmas morning and not be a child.
—ERMA BOMBECK

There is nothing quite as mean as giving a child a practical Christmas present.
—LENORE HERSHEY

If you got everything you wanted for Christmas where would you put it.
—UNKNOWN

Always believe in Santa. Just be-Claus.
—UNKNOWN

Christmas is the only time of year that you can get homesick even when you are at home.
—EDWARD W HOWE

He who does not have Christmas in his heart will not find it under the tree.
—ROY L. SMITH

The best of all Christmas gifts around the tree is the presence of a happy family wrapped in each other.
—DALAI LAMA

There has only been one Christmas. The rest are anniversaries.
—MATT GROENING

One of the most glorious of all messes in the world is the mess created in the living room on Christmas Day. Don't clean it up too quickly.
—ANDY ROONEY

Christmas is a necessity. There has to be one day of the year to remind us that we are here for something other than ourselves.
—ALEXANDER SMITH

It's Christmas in the hearts that puts Christmas in the air.
—ORIANTHI

Never worry about the size of your Christmas tree. In the eyes of a three year old, they are all 30 feet tall.
—UNKNOWN

FUNNY 2

Some people are like clouds. When they go away it's a lovely day.
—W. SOMERSET MAUGHAM

My fake plants died because I didn't pretend to water them.
—GEORGE BURNS

Life isn't about waiting for the storm to pass. It's about learning to drink wine in the rain.
—LEE IACOCCA

If a telemarketer calls, I give the phone to my three year old and tell him it's Santa Claus.
—UNKNOWN

Yes officer I saw the speed limit sign but I didn't see you.
—UNKNOWN

Do fat drug dealers sell diet coke.
—UNKNOWN

You are not too drunk if you can lie on the floor without holding on.
—DEAN MARTIN

Women like silent men. They think we are listening.
—PROVERB

Everybody is someone else's weirdo.
—UNKNOWN

The shin bone is a part of the human body designed to find furniture in the dark.
—RULE OF LIFE

I have enough money to last me the rest of my life unless I buy something.
—JACKIE MASON

A good speech is like a woman's skirt. Short enough to get your interest but long enough to cover the essentials.
—JOHN LOVETT

Am I getting older or are the supermarkets playing better music.
—UNKNOWN

Sex after the age of 90 is like trying to play pool with a rope.
—UNKNOWN

It isn't premarital sex if you don't plan on getting married.
—UNKNOWN

Never do anything you don't want to explain to the paramedics.
—UNKNOWN

A day without sunshine is…night.
—STEVE MARTIN

We have enough youth. How about a fountain of smart.
—SOPHIA LOREN

3 out of 4 people make up 75% of the population.
—UNKNOWN

A good listener is a good talker with a sore throat.
—KATHERINE WHITEHORN

Raisins that look like chocolate chips are the reason I have trust issues.
—UNKNOWN

Not being able to sleep at night is a real eye opener.
—PROVERB

If it wasn't for Thomas Edison, we'd all be watching tv in the dark.
—NEWT GINGRICH

Be a "Fruit Loop" in a world of "Cheerios".
—UNKNOWN

Your pants will never get too tight if you don't wear any.
—UNKNOWN

My home town is so small that we don't have a town drunk. We all just take turns.
—GEORGE BURNS

If rum doesn't fix it, you're not using enough rum.
—UNKNOWN

Don't be mad at lazy people. They didn't do anything.
—AGATHA CHRISTIE

Carrots may be good for your eyes but, booze will double your vision.
—UNKNOWN

What happens if you get scared to death, twice.
—EARL WILSON

Burnt pizza, frozen beer and pregnant women are all consequences of not taking it out in time.
—UNKNOWN

I want to lose 10 pounds this year. Only 13 to go.
—JOAN RIVERS

A meeting without food should have been an email.
—UNKNOWN

If everyday is a gift then today is socks.
—UNKNOWN

My spouse thinks I'm crazy but I'm not the one who married me.
—BRITT EKLAND

I started with nothing and still have most of it left.
—MAHATMA GANDHI

Irony is the opposite of wrinkly.
—UNKNOWN

The older I get, the earlier it's late.
—UNKNOWN

Be careful when you follow the masses, sometimes the "m" is silent.
—INDIRA GANDHI

I can't walk on water but I can stagger on beer.
—CHRISTOPHER LEACH

Never make snow angels in a dog park.
—PROVERB

You can't drink all day unless you start in the morning.
—DEAN MARTIN

Practice safe sex. Always use condiments.
—GARY SHANDLING

Ladies, don't hula hoop without a bra on.
—JOAN RIVERS

I'm almost a millionaire. I have all the zeroes, now I need the one.
—UNKNOWN

My wife ask me to stop being a flamingo so, I had to put my foot down.
—DAVE WEINBAUM

Go braless, it will pull the wrinkles out of your face.
—JOAN RIVERS

It's so hot today that the cows are giving powdered milk.
—FARMER BROWN

My neighbor just yelled at her kids so loud that I brushed my teeth and put on my pj's.
—UNKNOWN

My fear of moving stairs is escalating.
—MITCH HEDBERG

Bread is like the sun. It rises in the yeast and sets in the waist.
—UNKNOWN

Some days are just a waste of deodorant.
—ELIZABETH TAYLOR

Do fleas ever wonder if there is life on other dogs.
—RITA RUDNER

I can rise and shine but not at the same time.
—UNKNOWN

I had my patience tested. I'm negative.
—JOAN RIVERS

The only thing that travels faster than light is weekends.
—JOHN SHIRLEY

Don't judge me until you have flown a mile on my broom.
—UNKNOWN

Today I broke my personal record for days lived.
—ADAGE

You only live once. Lick the bowl.
—NIKITA KHRUSHCHEV

Screaming "Oh God" in bed on Sunday morning does not constitute going to church.
—BOB NEWHART

Having a two year old is like running your blender without the lid on.
—EVERY MOM

Is an argument between two vegans still called a "beef".
—UNKNOWN

Guys with an eye patch and three fingers sell the best fireworks.
—UNKNOWN

I'm retired. Do it yourself.
—ME

My wife never complained until I got hearing aids.
—GROUCHO MARX

It isn't drinking alone if your dog is home.
—UNKNOWN

Be careful stirring the pot. Sometimes you might end up having to lick the spoon.
—ERIC HOFER

Telling a woman to calm down is like trying to baptize a cat.
—UNKNOWN

Maybe everyone has amnesia, but forgot.
—STEVEN WRIGHT

That's a horrible idea. What time do we start.
—GILBERT SELDES

It took a lot of willpower but I finally gave up dieting.
—JOAN COLLINS

Mumbling is the glue that holds every marriage together.
—KATHERINE HEPBURN

If you look close enough, the high horse most people are riding is really a donkey.
—THE TALMUD

The toes that you step on today may be connected to the butt you have to kiss tomorrow.
—PROVERB

Can you be a closet claustrophobic.
—UNKNOWN

Try to explain counterclockwise to a kid with a digital watch.
—JOSHUA COHEN

Isn't it too bad we don't retain as much of what we read as what we eat.
—JOE DAVIS

Masseurs are people who knead you.
—UNKNOWN

Before you borrow money from a friend, decide which you need more.
—JEAN CHATZKY

Of course I'm an organ donor. Who wouldn't want a piece of this.
—MY FAVORITE T-SHIRT

The difference between meditation and daydreaming…is drooling.
—HUGH JACKMAN

HE WHO LAUGHS, LASTS.
—ADAGE

ACKNOWLEDGEMENTS

I hope you enjoyed looking through my "labor of love" and at some point you smiled, cried, remembered a loved one or laughed out loud.

There are a few people that need special thanks. My wife, who was my spellcheck buddy and my biggest supporter. Max, I spent numerous days at the computer, and sometimes cursing it, when I should have been doing other things around the house. Thanks.

A blanket thank you to everyone at Friesen Press for all your support answering my silly questions and pointing me in the right direction every step of the way in a professional manner. You have became friends. Thank You.

To my family who helped amass the list whether you realized it or not (you will appreciate the front cover).

Last but certainly not least, thanks to all of you for purchasing this bit of coffee table material.

You have all helped make a dream come true.

DON'T QUOTE ME BUT...THANK YOU.

Rich

Printed in Canada